MICHAEL COLMER

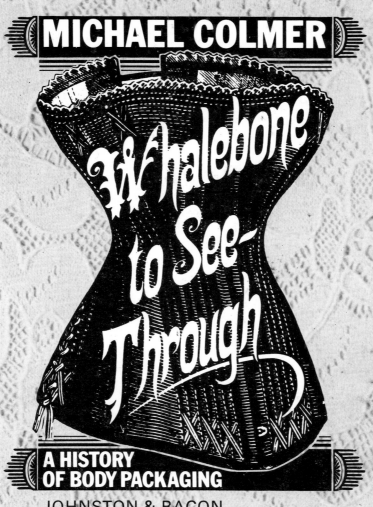

Whalebone to See-Through

A HISTORY OF BODY PACKAGING

JOHNSTON & BACON
LONDON · EDINBURGH

ACKNOWLEDGEMENTS

My sincere gratitude to all those individuals and companies who were generous enough to assist me with their time and their resources in compiling this tribute to the history of feminine body packaging especially; Keith Ascough, Tom Blumenau, Eric Cunliffe, Sheila Gore, Kay Haverfield, Helen W. Jones, Verne L. King, Milton J. Kristt, Dennis Lutchford, Georgina Picano, Patsy Randall, Peter Reger. Berlei; Du Pont, London, New York & Frankfurt; Fiorucci; Gossard; Lily of France; Motorway Tyres; Penthouse; Pirelli; Janet Reger; Silhouette; Warnaco.

Other illustrations were supplied by the BBC Picture Library, The Mander & Mitchenson Collection; Robert Harding & Associates and from the authors own archives.

My thanks also to the ever helpful staffs of the Victoria & Albert Museum and the British Museum in London and the Public Library and the Metropolitan Museum in New York and 'Intimate Fashion News' in New York.

For my son James Philip John, in the hopes that he might be better prepared than his father.

A JOHNSON & BACON book published by Cassell Ltd.
35 Red Lion Square,
London WC1R 4SG
and Tanfield House, Tanfield Lane,
Edinburgh EH3 5LL
and at Sydney, Auckland, Toronto, Johannesburg
an affiliate of
Macmillan Publishing Co.
New York

First Published 1979

ISBN 0 7179 4252 X

Designed by James Campus

Printed and Bound in Great Gritain by Morrison & Gibb Ltd;
Edinburgh and London.

BIBLIOGRAPHY

Readers who might like to study this subject in a little more depth would enjoy;
The History of Lingerie
MDC Crawford & EG Crawford
Fairchild Publications, New York 1952

The Strouse, Adler Story
Strouse, Adler Company, New Haven Connecticut, 1962

The Corset
Benedict Zilliacus
Oy Sjoblom Ab Finalnd and Ab Corsett-Industry Sweden 1963

The Future out of the Past
Arthur W. Pearce
The Warner Brothers Company
Bridgeport, Connecticut 1963

In our Own Fashion
R. & W. H. Symington Company of Market Harborough and the Harley Publishing Company, London 1956

Fashion in Underwear
Elizabeth W. Ewing
B. T. Batsford, London 1971

The Unfashionable Human Body
Bernard Rudoksky
Doubleday & Company, New York, 1971

INTRODUCTION

If I were allowed to chose from the books that will be published 100 years after my death . . . I would simply take up a fashion magazine so that I could see how women dress one century after my departure. Because these rags would tell me more about future humanity than all the philosophers, novelists, prophets and scholars. *Anatole France (1844-1924)*

IT'S BEEN FIVE THOUSAND YEARS SINCE woman first pulled knickers over her thighs, four thousand since she squeezed into corsets to proclaim her waistline and three thousand years since she first sported a brassière to contain her breasts.

But, curiously, it has only been in the last 100 years that such garments have become an essential part of her armoury of charms and only five decades since her mate has been permitted to know anything of the fabricated enigma that lies beneath the ever-fluctuating outer package he adores as woman. Even today, at the dawn of the 1980s, mere man will make his seasonal pilgrimage to the sanctum of the lingerie floor of the stylish department stores in search of that little black frothy something and display his dutiful naïveté as to the size of his lover's waist or bust.

Unburdened by the need to support his flat hairy chest and unconcerned – with the exception of a few historical hiccups – by the desire to censure his waistline, man has traditionally paid little heed to those dictates of undercover fashion and modesty that concern his sister. Indeed for his own part he is happily content to surrender his own measurements to the woman in his life, be she mother or wife, in order that she may clothe his limbs by way of the glossy catalogues of Sears Roebuck and the Great Universal Stores or over the chain store counters of Korvettes and Marks & Spencer.

One exception to this masculine indifference occurred in the eighteenth century; 'They say the Prince has left off his stays and that Royalty divested of its usual supports makes a bad figure', declared Lord Holland in 1817 of the bulky heir to the throne of England who resorted to corsetry to help him achieve the vogue of the 26-inch waist.

Another curiosity, the codpiece, began as the armoured case by which man protected his most precious jewel in battle. Adopted by the commoner as a leather support it enjoyed a fashionable revival in the sixteenth century as a gaudy pouch of padded silk, but, if we are to believe the *American Dictionary of Costume* 'This container served to hold money, handkerchief and sometimes bonbons'. It still survives today, albeit in a plasticised translation, as the jock strap, a protective masculine support in horse racing and aggressive sports like ball games. (A more tenuous derivative appeared in the mid-sixties in the form of 'cross your groin' underpants for men.)

But beyond the simple functions of warmth and comfort man is not concerned with his own underwear, seeing it merely as one of the five or six layers of clothing which encase the masculine stomach pit. Conversely he is, and always has been, fascinated with the hidden artifice employed by women to suppress and conceal or boost and reveal her body.

This is a notable reversal of roles with our fellow creatures, for in the animal kingdom it is the male of the species who entices

'Nature's full proportions' were the epitome of grace and queenly bearing at the turn of the century. This advertisement, from the mail order catalogue of the giant Sears, Roebuck Company of Chicago, appeared in 1908. In 1880 one leading American corsetry manufacturer spent $4.7m in advertising revenue. By 1890 the figure had risen to $29m and by 1900 it had soared to $50m.

his mate by the splendour of his display. But in human society it is the female who, on reaching that moment in her life when a secret atavism endows her with the pride of her sex, sets out to allure by changing her marketing-mix by every means open to her, be it a constant parade of clothing or colour, a false hairstyle in the form of a wig or cosmetic artifice to create illusion. Thus, in the battle of the sexes in which her clothes are her offensive weapons, woman sees nothing wrong in wearing hidden clothes specifically designed to enhance her shape.

1896
Curved Front
anchored at the waist

1900
Straight Front
a new fashion begins

1903
Hose Supporter Corset
anchored on the hips

1906
The Narrowest Waist
deep gores at the hips

1909
The Longer Look
hips are getting slimmer

1910
Natural Waistline
the hip line is smooth

1913
An Elegant Bra
more and more popular

1917
Front Lace Corset
still firm and long

1919
A New Look
the end of an era

The shape of a woman's body as it might have looked had it moulded to the shape of the clothes of four different periods. *Left :* 1913 and the hobble skirt. *Centre left :* 1870 and embustled. *Centre right :* 1904 the structured monobosom and *(right)* the 1920 flapper. A series of plaster figures, modelled by Costantino Nivola for their designer, Professor Bernard Rudofsky, which appeared at his exhibition entitled 'Are clothes modern?' held at the New York Museum of Modern Art in 1944.

BEFORE THE SEWING MACHINE

IT IS DIFFICULT, IN AN ERA OF SOPHISTICATED media, to imagine a time when fashion was the sole prerogative of the eccentric. Accustomed as we are to the fashion pages of our daily newspapers, the proliferation of women's magazines crammed with fashion comment, and such books as this, it takes mental agility to visualise a time before the invention of the sewing machine, paper patterns, mail order, high-street chain stores, standard sizes, French couturiers, man-made fibres and cheap Korean labour.

For the Greeks, Persians, Assyrians and Hebrews the concept of fashion presented no problem; it didn't exist. Their draped outer clothing was unisex and the sole requirements were necks, shoulders and waists as points of attachment. But for the historian bent on revealing underwear the origins are impossible to look up or pin down.

A terracotta figurine of a female athlete, dating from 3000 BC and now preserved in the Louvre in Paris, offers the first clue. Apart from its necklace, the only clothing on this carving is a pair of bikini briefs. It's easy to surmise that this garment was born out of chafing frustration with the ubiquitous loincloth drawn up between the legs but the next point of reference requires a breathtaking leap of 1000 years and a visit to the British Museum in London to see statuettes of bare-breasted Cretan women in fully laced corsets. After this important development there comes another frustrating vacuum but thanks to those early Greek fashion scribes like Homer in the eighth century BC, and Herodotus in 450 BC, we learn of the *zone*, a girdle of linen worn around the waist and hips to hold the garment and the first brassière, which, despite confusion as to whether it was known as the *apodesmos* or the *mastodeton*, we do know was made from soft leather or linen and worn around the bust to minimise it.

The Romans kept the garments but not the names. The girdle became a *cestus* and the bra, called a *strophium,* was still worn to

Illustrations on this, and facing page, courtesy Robert Harding Associates.

restrain rather than enhance the bouncing bosom. That familiar 'bikini girl' mosaic of fourth-century Sicily is not a sunbather but an athlete.

Despite the wealth of artistic output that has survived from this period, the nature of underwear remains a mystery and it was not until the seat of the mighty Roman Empire moved to Constantinople in the fourth century AD that we find a major fashion influence; the use of trousers. At first the Romans eschewed the ugly breeches as the mark of the barbarian; but the armies of the Empire, forced to fight and serve in colder climates, adopted the trouser. These baggy bifurcates were eventually to become men's underpants and women's knickers, and the loose-fitting tunic of this period later developed into the shirt and the chemise.

From the fourth to the eleventh century, after the Romans withdrew their cohorts to protect their beleaguered homelands, leaving their European colonies defenceless, illustrative records are rare. From the eleventh to the thirteenth century the Crusades preoccupied Europe. When the Franks eventually withdrew from Syria in 1291, Europe had become a very different place. A spirit of romantic heroism had been born, and fresh influences were everywhere: new foods, new colours and new fashions; lilac and purple, cotton, muslin, damask – even the glass mirror – all flooded into Europe from the East. The Crusaders also brought back with them the Muslim concepts of femininity. Eurowoman discarded her shapeless robes, her long loose tunics began to be laced closer to her body to display form, shape and charms, a development which was eventually to become a separate garment, the bodice.

So began woman's obsession with her waistline and soon garments were to be cut in shapes to enhance this discovery of the figure. Two layers of linen, stiffened with paste, became an under-bodice or tunic, described by the French as a *cotte,* and was the origin of the corset. It was later to be known as a *body* and later still the *stay.*

But strapping the ribs was not enough: to emphasise a small waist, skirts became wider and sleeves fuller – and here the royal courts of Europe led the way. From Spain, after the marriage of Philip II to the English Queen, Mary, in 1554, came the solution to the copious skirts which inhibited freedom for the legs – the Spanish farthingale. This was an underskirt constructed of hoops of wire, wood or whalebone that grew wider towards the hemline.

From France, in 1580, came another version, the wheel farthingale, which encircled the waist and thence down to the

A fashionable enigma, the bare-breasted Cretan woman of 2000 BC in her fully laced corsets. Robert Harding Associates.

ground. Those who could not afford such expensive courtly fashions used the *bum roll,* a hip bolster contrived from a padded sausage of cloth tied around the waist by tapes. And from Spain again the final emphasis, the *busc* or busk, this was a simple oblong strip carved from wood, horn or ivory which was laced from waist to bosom to provide reinforcement to the stomacher which formed the front of the bodice.

This was undoubtedly one of the most masochistic periods in the whole history of women's undergarments. That royal doyenne of fashion, Catherine de Medici, wife of Henry II of France, proscribed the thick torso and prescribed an ideal waist measurement of thirteen inches, a dictate which may have been responsible for the hinged iron corset of that period. This rigid construction of the female shape continued into the seventeenth century, defying political change as Charles I lost his head to the Lord Protector, Oliver Cromwell. In fact, though the Puritan régime condemned the fripperies of the Cavaliers it commended the use of strict figure control for women on the grounds that it encouraged body discipline, an attitude that brought scorn from its opponents and the epithets 'staid' and 'straight-laced' into the dictionary.

But Cromwell died in 1658, his son Richard was dismissed and two years later Charles II was on the throne, bringing with him the French fashions of his exiled court. The monarchy restored a profusion of silks, velvets, lace, bows and ribbons, and the stiffened bodice gave way to stays reaching from waist to underarm. The stiffening agent was now whalebone, in use since the twelfth century for strengthening head-dresses. In the interests of fashion the poor whale was being helped on his way to extinction.

The end of the seventeenth century saw the introduction of hoops and panniers; similar to the Elizabethan farthingale, these were constructions designed to exaggerate the hip and minimise the waist. This is a fashion that is popular with the illustrators of children's books, and many a 'Mary, Mary quite contrary' and 'Little Miss Muffet' sports the mob cap, panniered skirt and full petticoat of this era.

Despite the hoops and petticoats it was essential to wear a stay in order to achieve a really slim waist. Hesitantly the women's magazines began to publish instructions for making stays, so readers might make their own. Those who could afford it, went to a stay-maker, who quickly became as important as a hairdresser to any self-respecting lady of fashion. Every large town had its stay-maker but the most famous was undoubtedly Cosins of London whose fittings had something of a sacred ceremony about them.

Such was the grip of the stay in the Western world at the beginning of the eighteenth century that when Lady Mary Wortley Montagu, wife of the English ambassador to Constantinople, visited a Muslim bath house she reported:

'The lady that seemed the most considerable among them entreated me to sit with her, and would have fain undressed me for the bath. I excused myself with difficulty. They being however so earnest in persuading me, I was at last forced to open my shirt and shew them my stays, which satisfied them very well; for, I saw they believed I was locked up in that machine, and that it was not in my power to open it, which contrivance they attributed to my husband.'

The Muslim women had concluded quite correctly that European women were locked into oversized chastity belts, but had assumed incorrectly that this was a device thrust upon wives by their men. The eagerness with which women welcomed the stay's embrace is only one of those mysteries that abound in the world of fashion. These were dramatic days. In his *Anthropometamorphosis*

Another historical curiosity, the Ceinture de Chasteté – or Chastity Belt. This example made from steel was displayed at the Cluny Museum in Paris in 1910. According to some sources and contrary to popular belief, this strange 'garment' was worn as defensive protection rather than a symbol of masculine possession.

of 1653 the learned Dr John Bulwer had declaimed upon exposure of the female breast:

'Too many ladies among us, who by opening these common shops of temptation, invite the eyes of every chapman to cheapen that flesh which seems to lie exposed (as upon an open stall) to be sold.' Aghast that such women should 'parade their udders', he implored them to shut up shop and 'translate their masques from their face to their breast'. Twenty years later, the French priest Abbé Jacques Boileau published a book *A Just and Seasonable Reprehension of Naked Breasts and Shoulders* in which he warned that 'the sight of a beautiful bosom is as dangerous as that of a basilisk'.

Perhaps these disapproving declarations were prompted by occasional lapses of behaviour in court society. The most famous example being the appearance of a certain Miss Chudleigh, one of the Maids of Honour at the Court of the Prince of Wales, at a grand Jubilee ball in the summer of 1749. Miss Chudleigh chose to grace the party in the character of the chaste Iphigenia, ready for sacrifice in a dress that was slashed to the waist. Also at that ball was the intrepid Lady Mary Wortley Montagu, who was heard to remark with enviable acidity that the High Priest would have no difficulties in inspecting the entrails of the victim. Ten years later a respected physician was to declare against yet another female 'fetish'. According to the good Dr Willicks; 'In high life many women and girls now wear drawers, an abominable invention which produces disorders in abundance.'

In 1790 a fashion revolution arrived from France that matched the political upheavals. The famous dressmaker, Rose Bertin, fled the Revolution to the safety of England, where she imperiously condemned strict body control in favour of the Empire Line. This

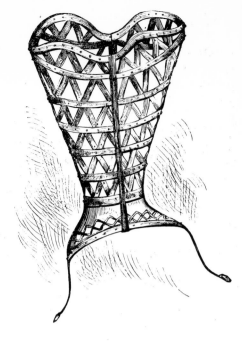

Above : An Elizabethan 'body' of steel, leather and whalebone to mould the waist and support the farthingale.

Opposite page, above right : Another steel corset and although its hinged flaps suggest it was used to support the panniered dresses of the seventeenth century some authorities believe that these 'iron maidens' were worn for health reasons.

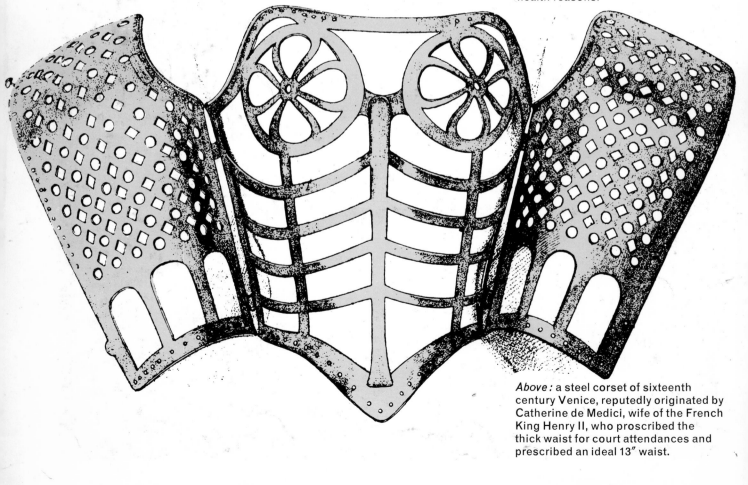

Above : a steel corset of sixteenth century Venice, reputedly originated by Catherine de Medici, wife of the French King Henry II, who proscribed the thick waist for court attendances and prescribed an ideal 13″ waist.

was the new fashion of a new Republic; members of the Directoire had looked back to the first republic of ancient Greece for their political and social inspiration and alongside democratic reform came a revival of Greek costume. The rigid hoops, stays and panniers supporting multi-coloured silks and satins were swept away, and in their place high-waisted muslin or cotton shifts, dampened to cling to the body, were worn with shorter hair, flat slippers, and flesh-coloured tights to give an illusion of nudity. But whilst diaphanous muslin may have been suitable for ancient Greece it did have disadvantages in the colder English climate. Those who had dampened their dresses to accentuate their contours put their health at risk. This, combined with the views of those women whose fuller figures were not seen to best advantage in the unfettered state, put an end to the Empire Line. By 1810 a lighter boned waist-corset was in use and by 1821 the heavier, fully whaleboned version had returned, complete with tight lacing and the first attempts at providing cup-shaped bust sections to replace the unyielding busk. One such development separated the hitherto single entity by means of a padded triangle of metal; it was known as 'the divorce corset'.

But all these garments were unique, either handcrafted around those who could afford them or home-made by those who could not. Fashion had dictated figure shape and every woman wanted to be fashionable. Thus the scene was set for the arrival of the mass produced garments which would bring figure control – albeit without comfort – within the reach of every woman.

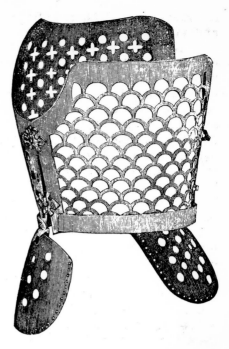

Below : Madame Pompadour sports the Turkish trouser dress which Amelia Bloomer was to promote unsuccessfully in America and Europe in the 1850s.

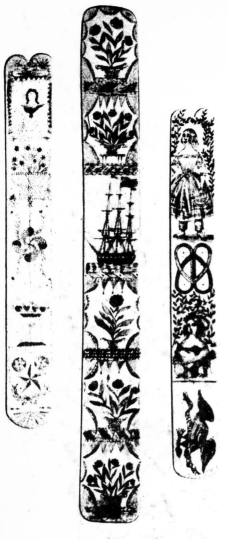

Examples of decorated whalebone busks from the collection at Mystic Seaport, Connecticut which for many years was one of the home ports of the East coast whale hunting fleets. The busk slotted into early corsets and was tightly laced to stiffen the bust. A highly romantic and daring gift the busk was, like the fan, a mock weapon that nimbly cracked many an over-eager masculine knuckle.

'The marvellous effect of Lacing' a French cartoon of 1813. By far the loudest cries raised in defence of the vice-like grip of laced corsetry came from the wearers themselves. Womens' magazines on both sides of the Atlantic hotly debated the burning issue. Mothers saw nothing wrong in lacing their growing daughters into the tightest garment they could find. But by 1837 (right) Paris had called a halt to the torture as this simple satin corset shows. Radio Times Hulton Picture Library.

Whilst Western civilisation has always regarded the bust-reservoirs de la maternité – as sacrosanct many peoples, like these Kenyan maidens, still retain sufficient respect for its sight to take it for granted, although both underwear manufacturers and missionaries have done their best to correct this apparent lack of prejudice. *Robert Harding Associates.*

MASS PRODUCTION

APRIL 1855 NOT ONLY brought spring to Victorian England, but also a fashion revolution that was to sweep through Europe and on to the Colonies. The Court page of *The Times* duly recorded that Napoleon III accompanied by his wife, the Empress Eugénie, visited Her Majesty Queen Victoria at Windsor Castle; but the society pages revealed the dramatic effect of that meeting. The Empress sported a new fashion which captured the hearts of man and the envy of women: the crinoline.

The crinoline cage of 1860.

Admittedly the word 'crinoline' had been in use for over twenty-five years; taken from the French word for horsehair, *crin*, and the latin for thread, *linum,* it meant a short petticoat. The crinoline worn by Eugénie was a full grey skirt trimmed with black lace and pink bows and it achieved instant popularity, not only because of its regal endorsement but because its lightweight cage-construction freed women from the weight and bulk of yards of muslin, calico and flannel. It swept across the rigid social barriers of the Victorian era and was soon worn by society women as well as the new middle-class wives of merchants and traders, the fettered factory workers and country peasants (in spite of the difficulties it caused on the workbench).

The crinoline, with its emphasis on a slim waist, demanded the tightest control of the figure and that spelt 'corset' writ exceedingly large, especially for the fashionably ample bosom of the Victorian era. Such was the demand that the 100,000 seamstresses slaving twelve-hour shifts in appalling conditions simply could not cope. Early attempts to replace hand labour by machines had proved desultory, but now the need for mechanisation was urgent.

One example of the growth of a corsetry company from cottage trade to corporation lies in the romantic history of W. H. Symington.

At the age of nineteen, James Symington left his Scottish home to follow his brother to the sleepy Leicestershire town of Market Harborough, one hundred landlocked miles north of London. Brother William opened a grocery shop and James moved next door to set up in business as a tailor, hatter and woollen draper. Two years later William moved to a neighbouring town and larger factory premises; occupants of the empty property next door were Mrs Gold and her daughter Sarah, both skilled stay-makers.

Within three years James Symington married the girl next door, adding the craft of stay-making to his billheads, and settled down to a prosperous future and a large family. In 1850 he leased a cottage with a yard, off the High Street, and Sarah was wringing miracles of fine sewing and embroidery from her three seamstresses, from six o'clock in the morning to ten o'clock at night.

And then in 1855, the same year that the Empress Eugénie had displayed her crinoline to the Queen, William and Sarah's eldest son Robert announced his departure for the Colonies at the adventurous age of eighteen. Incredibly in a New World, where so many of his fellow countrymen were enthusiastically sharing in the growing pains of an expanding young nation, Robert Symington did *not* prosper, and within a year he was back. But the Symington entrepreneurial eye did not entirely fail him, for on his travels he had met an inventor called Isaac Singer who was then trying to convince his fellow Americans that he had perfected a sewing-machine which worked unfailingly. He had little difficulty in convincing young Master Robert who immediately recognised the potential of this device in the family business. Thus three of Mr Singer's treadle machines made the 4000-mile journey across the Atlantic to the little English town of Market Harborough.

Sarah Symington shared her son's enthusiasm but her seamstresses, now increased to six, did not; they all refused to work these devilish contraptions. The redoubtable Sarah prevailed, however, and the first mechanised corset factory in England was in production by 1856.

American women had to suffer the cost of imported corsets for another five years—or make their own from hand-woven bleached cotton, quilt-stitched around whalebone stiffeners—before the persistent Mr Singer had achieved his objective. In 1861 two men set up sewing machines in New Haven, Connecticut for the manufacture of 'unmentionables', and this partnership grew into the Strouse Adler Company, which, together with another firm, the Royal Worcester Company, began the American foundation garment industry. It was no accident that these two companies sprang up in New England, for the vital ingredient, whalebone, was readily available here. The prosperity of a number of maritime communities along the Atlantic seaboard depended on this fashion.

Some social historians have tried to suggest that these corsets were man's last attempt to keep woman helplessly bound to the home, in constant fear of fainting. But by far the loudest cries raised in defence of the vice-like grip of corsetry came from the wearers themselves, adding fuel to a controversy that was to last over seventy years. Women's magazines on both sides of the Atlantic hotly disputed this burning issue. Mothers saw nothing wrong in lacing their growing daughters into the tightest garment they could find, aided, no doubt, by a determined foot on the spine. Readers spoke proudly of waists as narrow as fourteen inches, dismissing pain in the interests of vanity.

Such was the popularity of both corset and crinoline that an attempt to release women from their self-inflicted torture—and perhaps the first example of a fashion influence reaching Britain from America—failed when the editor of the fashion magazine *Lily*, Mrs Amelia Bloomer, appeared in a Turkish trouser dress. This consisted of baggy trousers, gathered at the ankles, and a voluminous skirt down to the knees modelled very closely on the dress worn by Turkish women, save that the trousers, sleeves and skirt were decidedly not transparent.

Despite its modesty and promise of freedom, Mrs Bloomer won

Electricity was a newly discovered enchantment to the Victorians. Men could enjoy a few healthy jolts of electrical energy from machines in amusement arcades and even purchase 'virility belts' to encompass their groin for the same purpose. Women were offered electric corsets whose magnetism came from the metallic composition of the garment.

The first advertisement placed in 1875 by Lucien C. Warner and I. De Ver Warner, two young American physicians appalled at the anatomical dangers of contemporary corsetry, in 'Peterson's Fashion Magazine', a year after the Warner company began.

little more than that polite English 'How curious'. And so that militant mouthpiece of American feminity returned home a sadder woman, unaware that she had bequeathed to the English language that word for women's baggy bifurcates which, until recently, could always be relied upon to raise a vaudeville snigger.

Her reception in America was a little more pointed; several Bloomer pioneers suffered mob ridicule and such weighty pronouncements as the one in the *Medical Times* which proclaimed: 'The idea of females wearing trousers may be scouted as ridiculous'. The Bloomerites had lost the day, although within fifty years they were to some degree vindicated when one august American women's journal wrote in 1895: 'Let it not be understood that the bloomer should be sanctioned on ordinary occasions; it is neither necessary nor pretty on the street, and does not look well in the drawing-room, but for bicycling it is admirable and nothing can take its place.'

But with the flurry in the dovecot resolved in the mid-nineteenth century, women on both sides of the Atlantic returned to the sanctity of the crinoline. Some indication of how much it was revered comes from the pen of George Bernard Shaw, writing in the unlikely role of fashion commentator for *McCall's Magazine*:

'I shall never forget the shock I received when, on walking into our parlour one day without the least preparation, I first saw a lady without a crinoline. She seemed to me a monster, incredible, impossible, revolting, indecent. I was old enough not to scream and run away and even to pretend that the universe still proceeded normally . . .' Having a figure then meant having a waist like an hourglass or wasp. It was reported that the most devoted and resolute followers of this fashion lay flat on their faces on the floor, whilst their maids placed one foot in the small of their backs so as to get the most powerful possible purchase for pulling the laces and achieving the utmost constriction possible without cutting the lady in two. There was vigorous propaganda against tight lacing, with fearful pictures of the disablement of the internal organs. These pictures produced no effect whatever.

In 1874 two young American physicians, Lucien T. Warner and I. De Ver Warner became so alarmed at the 'disablement of the internal organs' endured by their female patients that they invented a new garment. The following year a classified advertisement appeared in *Peterson's Fashion Magazine* for 'Dr Warner's Sanitary Corset' complete with Skirt Supporter and Self Adjusting Pads. For $1.50 the two Warner brothers of New York would send a sample of what they described as 'The only corset constructed upon physiological principles, securing health and comfort of body with grace and beauty of form'.

But, if the iron grip of the stay was to be relaxed, so too was the cult of the crinoline. By 1865 it had already lost its circular shape, recognised as a hazard in high winds, an anti-social garment in public places and an undoubted fire risk. It first altered to a flat front and then even lost its sides in favour of a curious cage strapped behind the waist; this was called a crinolette but was later to become known as the bustle as ingenious Victorian inventors vied with each other to create the perfect folding mechanism which would collapse when the wearer sat down.

The turn of the century was an exploding era of fashion, with prototypes becoming cults encouraged by the supreme authority of the proliferation of women's magazines and the newly emergent garment factories.

Abhorred as indecent prior to 1800, drawers were now commonly worn. Initially they were simply two flaps joined at the

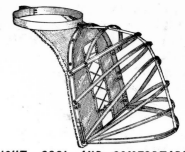

LIGHT, COOL AND COMFORTABLE.
The best Fifty Cent Folding Bustle in the market. It is recommended by fashionable ladies and leading dressmakers. PERFECT in shape and ADJUSTABLE in size. The improved folding principle used in this Bustle results in its always regaining its shape after pressure. It is the easiest and yet the most effective and durable spring ever presented. Its superior finish and elegant style make it a most desirable Bustle.

One of many attempts to overcome the restrictions of the bustle.

Closer to the brevity of the contemporary brassiére were these adjustable Victorian 'dress forms' braided in wire and covered in lace.

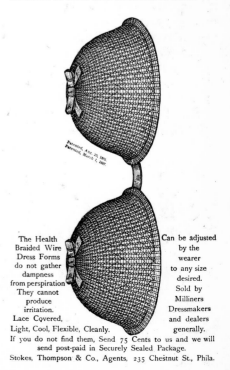

The Health Braided Wire Dress Forms do not gather dampness from perspiration They cannot produce irritation. Lace Covered, Light, Cool, Flexible, Cleanly.

Can be adjusted by the wearer to any size desired. Sold by Milliners Dressmakers and dealers generally.

If you do not find them, Send 75 Cents to us and we will send post-paid in Securely Sealed Package.
Stokes, Thompson & Co., Agents, 235 Chestnut St., Phila.

waistline on a tape, and made from pure white cotton. More daring ladies added black lace flounces for wear under dark skirts and, by the turn of the century, they became known as 'French knickers'.

The chemise, which had long been popular, won renewed acclaim when it was introduced as a one-piece garment incorporating drawers and described as 'combinations'.

And then there was the suspender. Unchivalrously displacing the garter twenty years before the end of the century, it began as a harness around the neck but rapidly descended the female form in its search of anchorage, hanging from the waistbelt by 1885 and finally finding a permanent home in 1900 dangling from the corset.

But undoubtedly the most innovative underwear design was the bust-bodice, heavily boned, of course, to maintain the fashionable monobosom which produced the curious S-shaped profile with the bust thrown forward and the bustle extending the trunk backwards. This was a style immortalised by the American artist Charles Dana Gibson who invented the 'Gibson girl' and called by some the 'Kangaroo Figure'.

The corset itself had changed too. Whalebone, proving to be of varying quality and speculative price, had been overtaken by the Mexican ixtle plant. Those enterprising Warner brothers had devised machinery for shaping the plant fibres into cords, sizing and tempering them to create 'an unbreakable exclusive boning material called Coraline'. Then a third Warner, son of one of the founders, working secretly with a steel wire manufacturer created rust-proof coated flat spring steel which replaced conventional stiffening materials and which was to prove highly profitable to the family business for ten years.

In a period of rapidly changing fashions such as the 1900s, corsetry manufacturers headed determinedly for Paris every season. Corsets were, after all, the foundation for clothes and, as the high priests of haute couture, Worth, Paquin, and especially Poiret, displayed their creations, the corsetiers watched with shrewd eyes. As autumn followed spring, the corset changed shape with the waistline, which was always on the move, in, out, up, down—never, never the same.

As corset tops dropped, the customary corset cover, a product of Victorian hypermodesty, no longer had a corset to cover. In 1902 the American Charles de Bevoise, made a form-fitting corset cover with built-in shoulders, named it the 'brassière' and sold it for stout women. Curiously this word has never been used by the French,

Warner Brothers' Coraline Corsets.

HEALTH CORSET,
WITH TAMPICO BUSTS.

Very comfortable, and gives an elegant form.

CORALINE CORSET.

Made of heavy satteen, with double steel. A favorite corset.

Flexible Hip Corset.

Warranted not to break over the hips. A great favorite with all ladies.

Adjustable Hip Corset.

Made adjustable to every figure, and of superior finish.

Mary Anderson writes:
I am delighted with your Coraline Corset. It is perfect in fit and elegant in design and workmanship.

✲FLEXIBLE HIP✲HEALTH✲NURSING✲

who describe this garment as a *soutien gorge*.

In the same year the two Warner brothers also made a tight-fitting bust supporter and quickly produced several types: long, short, hook-side, hook-back and crossover surplice back. The bust, with its own foundation garment, came into its own.

For those to whom nature had not been generous, magazines offered remedies, such as the consumption of half a dozen prunes every night. The giant Sears Roebuck mail order company of Chicago offered its own solution: the 'Princess' bust developer which, for $1.50, promised to 'Permanently develop and enlarge the bust, cause it to fill out to nature's full proportions, give that swelling, rounded firm white bosom, that queenly bearing, so attractive to the opposite sex. Transforms a thin, awkward unattractive girl or woman into an exquisitely formed, graceful, fascinating lady, positively without fail.' If for some strange reason the device did not work, money would be refunded—and customers no doubt advised to purchase that company's famous lace-trimmed muslin bust forms 'undetectable in use'.

The corset was now big business and advertising revenue grew with sales, the figures for one American manufacturer alone reveal that, whilst in 1880 the company spent $4.7m in advertising its corsetry, by 1890 the sum had risen to $29m and had soared to $50m by 1900.

Despite this promotional investment, women were still undecided whether they should stay with the traditional long-line corset or change to the shorter garment twinned with the new brassière. A trade magazine for July 1905 records the 'corset dilemma':

'Notwithstanding all the talk to the contrary, and a deal of advertising on the part of the trade converting the American woman to corset shapes as they are understood in Paris and London, the sales of the past few months have proved that the older style corset is as popular as ever, and the new model is, as yet, a complete stranger to many women who envince no wish or inclination for an introduction to or acquaintance with it.

'The correct height of the corset as formulated by the designers and approved by the vast majority of women is that which gives support to the bust without undue elevation. In other words, the corset top should reach halfway across the bust. This sounds the golden mean which is neither the extreme low bust of vulgar suggestion, nor the newly advocated high bust of uncomfortable contour. It is the one mostly in demand because it has been tried and weighed in the balance'.

Six months later a breathless reporter from the *Women's and Infants' Furnisher* revealed the latest news from Paris: 'French women of good taste do not wish to wear above a thin waist a garment that looks like a corset cover; that is, one with too much lace trimming or showing running strings of coloured ribbon. Yet the tight-fitting separate lining does not approach the ideal of feminine coquetry. The result has been a garment, a corset cover, or sometimes called a *maillot,* perfectly fitting, well supporting the bust and yet daintily trimmed. The best material is a linen batiste, thin yet wonderfully strong, and the decorations consist of embroidery, very fine and dainty but with very little open work, and a small use of narrow lace. The dainty touch to this garment is that it is perfectly finished over the hips, often in the form of little embroidered edge matching the décolletage which seems to take the garment far out of the province of a corset cover'.

The slogan 'A corset for every figure' revolutionised the trade and brought women to realise the value of figure control, generating an amazing multiplication of factories, an unprecedented number of corsetières, an enlargment of retail departments and a greater number of employees engaged in both wholesale and retail than might have seemed possible a decade earlier. Nor was the desire confined to any one class. In former years it had been the wealthy patron who had established the vogue of the imported model in America. She went in for things foreign and delighted in paying homage to the Parisian artists; she felt it to be a sort of link with sophisticated Europe and no price was considered too high to forge the link more securely. But, with corset education and the ill effects of corsets proven, even the average woman denied herself some outside glory or extravagance so that she could afford to enjoy that sweet assurance that in figure control she was all that the fashionable world approved.

But the niceties of high fashion wedded to entrepreneurial ability were not exclusive to America or Europe; in 1910 a young man called Fred Burley opened a corset factory in Australia (a dash of antipodean sensitivity prompted him to adopt 'Berlei' as his company's trading name). Burley was not Australia's first corsetier however. That claim went to Eleanor Hargreaves who, having been married at eighteen and twice widowed by the time she was thirty, maintained her four children by making women's under garments at 4s. 6d. a dozen in the gold-mining town of Ballarat in 1886. By 1894 her cottage had become a backyard factory with twelve treadle sewing machines and sixteen women employees; like Berlei, Eleanor (Hargreaves) Lucas was destined to grow.

Meanwhile, in Europe the war clouds gathered and burst forth upon the western world.

American corsets of the 1870s, made in a variety of materials; white or grey coutil, satin jean, English leather, black cashmere or heavy black, white and coloured silk. Fashionable magazines of the period determined that silk or cashmere corsets 'must be lined with jean and English leather with muslin.' On white and coloured corsets the seams were to be sewn with thread of white silk, black corsets with red silk. The final garment, *lower right*, was, in fact, a 'neglige' corset.

At the turn of the century corsetry manufacturers vied to prove that their garments were rustproof. The iron and steel supports that left their marks on the laundering of earlier garments were replaced by a coated flat spring steel pioneered by De Ver H. Warner, son of one of the founders of the Warner Brothers Company.

EMANCIPATION

IN THOSE BRIEF YEARS BETWEEN 1914 AND 1918 the First World War had as dramatic an effect upon fashion as it had on the political structure and resources of Europe and the strategy of America. Mobilisation of able-bodied men left pressing vacancies in essential services, and millions of women found themselves tackling jobs that would have seemed impossible before the war: munitions manufacture, factory assembly work, ambulance and heavy-vehicle driving as well as many other strenuous roles which demanded freedom of movement. This made the use of restrictive foundation garments out of the question. Steel and fabrics factories were turning their assembly lines to war time production, and corset manufacturers could not get the raw materials.

The period that followed hostilities marked the final emancipation of women on both sides of the Atlantic. One Victorian writer even commented that women had 'forsaken crying and fainting and taken up swearing and smoking'.

The House of Representatives had staunchly rejected the Women's Suffrage Amendment in 1915, but two years later it passed both Houses of Congress and was ratified by the necessary 36th State in 1919. A year earlier British women over thirty had won their franchise. The years of effort by women to achieve a greater degree of political, social and career freedom found their culmination in the right to vote—and the lid was off.

The suffragettes now freed from wartime factories, flexed their new-found feminine muscle in many ways, not the least of which was their desire to compete in sporting activities against and alongside their menfolk and this required much more freedom in both outer and inner clothing. A New York debutante, Mary Jacob, invented a soft brassière from two silk handkerchiefs tied with ribbon which she patented but later sold to the ambitious Warner brothers.

This was the signal for the corset manufacturers to enter the brassière market. The 'working girl' wanted to demonstrate her new equality with tailor-made costumes, short hair and a straight figure. Such was the economic power of this new market that the industry raced to provide her with brassières that were little more than tight bands of cotton suppressing the bosom in order to achieve the new boyish look.

The most amusing justification for this slim line came to light years later but, at the time, Paris, anxious to regain its pre-war authority in haute couture, set out to find a distinctive new look— and found it in Chanel's simple straight creations with short skirts. She decreed that breasts and waists were out, focusing all attention on the legs.

Years later it was suggested that the real reason for this revolutionary fashion was that French women, perturbed by the loss of thousands of Frenchmen at the Front, decided it was their patriotic duty to replenish the supply of Gallic manhood, and accordingly hoisted their skirts, abandoned their steel corsets and waistlines and became pregnant, comfortably, in a style which would draw eyes away from thickening waistlines. As history records the world followed suit and the 'Flapper' was born.

The war had also given impetus to the search for new fabrics,

Too shocking for Vogue!

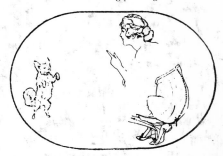

This passed Vogue's censor.

Warner's 'Natural Figure' advertising campaign appeared in 1914 and shocked both Vogue and the Boston Transcript into refusing to run the ads. To satisfy the censors the company removed everything possible except the actual garment. The result was both modest and sensational, bringing unexpected editorial tribute from such august publications as the New York Tribune and Harpers Weekly *(below)*.

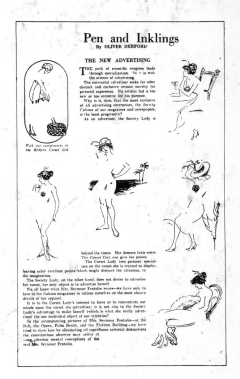

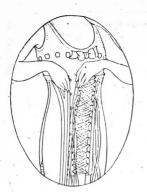

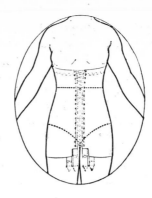

Gossard's instructions to sales staff on the correct method of adjusting corsets; 'Stand in front of your mirror and clasp the corset about the body, making sure that the lacing is directly at the centre front and the corset is low enough on the body, particularly at the back, to bring the waistline at the proper point and hug the figure at the hip bones. Fasten the front garters. Cross the lacings as shewn in the diagram and pull the corset smartly at the waistline. Commencing from the bottom of the clasp, lace up to the waistline, pulling the lacers with a downward tendency to prevent the corset from working up on the body. Then lace from the top of the corset down at the waistline. Go over this lacing two or even three times until the corset is properly adjusted. A correctly laced corset will show an even opening about 1½″ – never more than 2″ wide.'

and man-made textiles began to appear; the 1920s saw the invention of the corselette and the wrap-around made from a cloth rubber mixture worn next to the skin. This was a dramatic development because until then most women had worn corsets over a chemise or slip to keep it clean as laundering produced stains from the steel supports.

This post-war development was not without its tensions. The pace at which manufacturers expanded led to furious patent battles as each company fought to protect its garments from plagiarism. The public watched while the trade press sympathetically scooped up lucrative advertising pages packed with protests like the following 'hear this and tremble' admonition from Poirette Corsets Inc of New York City in 1926:

"Special Notice"

OUR FIRST SUIT for infringement brought against a large and prominent manufacturing corporation has been terminated by its COMPLETE AND UNRESTRICTED ACKNOWLEDGMENT OF OUR SOLE AND EXCLUSIVE OWNERSHIP OF **"COMPACT"** and the patent rights thereto under Patent No. 1,526,091 and the validity thereof.

LET THOSE who have been, are now, or contemplate manufacturing, selling or dealing in (either wholesale or retail) garments infringing upon our Patent rights take heed, as it is our purpose and intention to protect our rights to the full measure of the law.

Poirette
CORSETS
INC.
"HOME OF ORIGINATIONS"
11 EAST 26th STREET   NEW YORK CITY

The reason for corsetry patents, and their vehement protection against infringement, lay in the actual construction of the garments. A physical education instructor created the Tru-Balance corset which employed side sections cut on the cross and joined to a straight front panel following the line of the stomach muscles and lifting the abdomen. A civil engineer, tired of his wife's complaints, designed Warner's Sta-Up-Top which utilised bones knitted into the elasticated waistband to prevent it rolling over. La Resista's Nu-Back separated the back of the corset at waist level making it easier for the wearer to lean and stretch without pulling on her straps. Poirette's Mardi Bra had stitched appliqué ribbon trim from side seam to front strap and down to the centre front of the garment

THE MODERN VENUS IS CORRECTLY CORSETED

helping to divide and carry the weight of a large bust.

Eventually the manufacturers realised that the only real sufferers in this Battle of the Bulge Patent War were themselves and began to turn their attention to other forms of expansion. By 1921 Gossard, with offices in Chicago and New York, had spread north to Toronto, south to Buenos Aires, west to Sydney and east across the Atlantic, where the British H. W. Gossard Company was formed (Eight years later Fred Burley was to answer this invasion of foreign corsetiers into Australia by opening Berlei UK). Warners concluded licensing agreements with manufacturing companies in Canada, England, France, Belgium, Germany, Spain and Mexico.

Alongside American garments came the new marketing techniques, careful stock control, regular educational literature and training schools for departmental corsetières:

The advertising value of a neatly framed Gossard Diploma hanging in your corset department or displayed in your window cannot be over estimated. With a Gossard School Graduate in your store you should be able to secure 90 per cent of the desirable corset business in your community.

Just as exporting made mass production profitable—the same corset retailing for $8.50 in New York, cost £1 4s 3d in London in 1923 —the world of corsetry discovered that younger women no longer wanted to be fettered. Anxiously fighting to maintain their reluctant markets the manufacturers sought refuge in corselettes and increasingly lighter-weight undergarments in the hopes that they would appeal to the boyish flappers.

But the sales curve declined year by year, and by 1928 annual volume had been slashed to less than one-third of what it had been during the golden peak of 1920. The following year brought the Depression, and an even greater dip in sales with the threat of extinction for many companies.

The 1929 'Grand Street Follies' depicted a New York belle in the costume of a generation earlier, removing bustles, petticoats and old-fashioned drawers, chemises, corsets and bodices in such numbers that the audience held its breath as each garment was shed and uncovered not nudity but other bodices that only grandmother could name. The trade newspapers were appalled:

'It behoves the garment trade to take advantage of this form of exhibition and the time is ripe for action. It is only too evident when you hear the tumultuous laughter of the audience at the Follies, that it will not do to suggest heavy or constricting garments to the women of today, but clever and inventive stylists must use their wits to design undergarments which will help make the woman's figure show to the best possible advantage.

'No voluminous petticoats, constricting corsets or binding bodices. No buttons and buttonholes undercovers or flounces. The wardrobe of the young miss of today must hold in a cigar box. After her unconstrained sunbathed summer, she will not stand for heavy clothes that restrict her movements and make her feel hot and uncomfortable.'

In the grim atmosphere of survive-or-die, with vaudeville performers lampooning the great feminine gesture of 'yanking her corset', the larger manufacturers looked back to long-forgotten resources. Warners, recalling their innovative traditions, dismissed the existing bone, cloth and rubber corsets in search of a new material. They found it in Lastex from the United States Rubber Company, a soft, thin elastic webbing that stretched two ways and could be made into side panels joined to separate front panels. The corset could now stretch with body movements yet stay in place. Before long the new elastic fabrics were improved so that they could be used even in the cups of brassières.

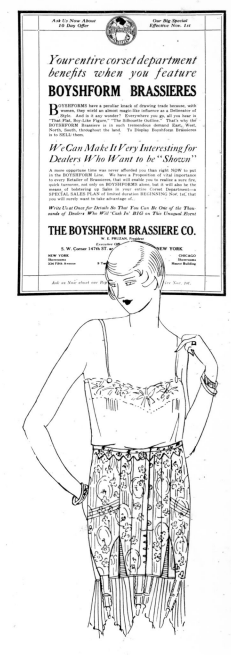

THE MODERN VENUS IS CORRECTLY CORSETED

FALL AND WINTER · 1927-28

This development caused Warners to examine the consumers' buying patterns. Research indicated that women of the same measurements around the bust needed different sized cups. These could be typed as: A: small, B: average, C: heavy, D: very heavy; this revolutionised brassière design, simplified retail stocks and assured wearers of a better fit. It also doubled sales for the industry and was soon adopted internationally.

The success of the new elasticated corset won universal praise. At a 'British Tea' reception held in New York in 1936 in honour of the English actress, Jeanne de Casalis, by the Charnoux Patent Corset Company the guest was suitably appreciative:

'In England you will not find a woman on the stage without a Charnoux. It is unheard of. You don't wear a corset, it becomes part of you and when you feel something wonderful you feel you must tell the world about it. Another thing about it is that it remains in place even without suspenders and it is the most hygienic thing you can possibly wear. Why, after wearing it in the theatre all day long I take it home, sponge it lightly with soap and water, powder it and put it on again. It feels as fresh and as new as if I had not worn it all day. It is the most exquisite thing to wear. I even wear it under a bathing suit.'

But barely had the industry recovered from the effects of one war, followed by the corset-shy flappers, and the Depression, when another blow descended upon them in the shape of the Second World War.

Some long-established European manufacturers apprehensively noted the approaching storm and did not wait to act. Max Lobbenberg and Emil Blumenau, having set up a corsetry company in Cologne, Germany, in 1887, had expanded the business to the point where they were employing a workforce of 400, specialising in corsetry for the fuller figure, bones, busks and rigid cloths.

As early as 1931 the Lobbenberg and Blumenau families had seen the growing power of the Nazi movement and moved the company to Paris to trade under a new name, 'Manufacture de Corsets Silhouette'. Their trademark was designed by one of the many unknown artists of Montmartre. By 1936 the new company was well established but so too was the threatening power of Nazi Germany, and for a second time the two families emigrated, this time to England to start afresh in North London where it took them four years to reach a turnover of £11,000, a sum that they had previously made in less than one day.

World war broke out, and for the second time in twenty years manufacturers were deprived of raw materials and their factories went into war production.

In Britain all clothing was rationed to coupon purchase and manufacturers limited to 'utility' styles. The restrictions influenced many facets of public and private life, and unexpected problems arose such as smaller newspapers and limited advertising space. But this did not stop the British Gossard company from declaring that it intended to be in business long after the war ended and, even though advertising space was limited, the company announced its intention to be conspicuous throughout the war in every well-read newspaper and periodical from Land's End to John O'Groats.

The restrictions were indeed daunting: cotton, rubber and steel went on the priority list for the war effort. Raw cotton, imported from America, Egypt and India was in short supply, enormous quantities being reserved for Government contracts. Rubber was lost when the Malayan rubber plantations fell to Japan in 1941, and synthetic rubber was in limited production for military needs. Steel was virtually impossible to obtain. In the five and a half years of the war the Gossard factory 'somewhere in England' turned out 348 experimental kites, 4113 convoy balloons, 19,000 life belts, 73,500 sails, 34,807 distress flags, 26,095 man-dropper parachute repairs, 98,700 dinghies and 639,306 parachutes. But the company did not have to sacrifice all its underwear-manufacturing capacity for alongside the war production and the limited number of civilian garments was an order for 117,688 brassières for the Women's Royal Naval Service.

American service women were luckier in being allowed to choose their own undergarments. At first the Women's Army Auxiliary Corps were issued with girdles and brassières along with bathrobes, pyjamas and uniforms. But then the research technologist for the WAAC Quartermaster's Depot announced the conclusion that 'choosing a foundation was like choosing cosmetics, a very personal thing', and the WAACs acquired the right to choose their own.

Despite fashion magazine warnings to American women at the outbreak of the war that they had better hang on to their girdles because of a potential rubber shortage, the National War Board ruled that corsets were essential and allotted to the industry a sufficient quantity of steel for them to continue normal production. But not only corsets and brassières issued from the assembly lines, such items as cartridge boxes, flare parachutes, fragmentation bomb parachutes and tow-targets were also turned out. At least the American industry was saved the fate of British companies like Silhouette, who took pity on their staff and forsook the bomb-ravaged capital for new premises: a parish hall and a disused pub next to a prison in the west Midlands.

The summer of 1946 came in with a fanfare of trumpets and London was gay with pageantry. The mood was one of rejoicing for every industry. The Victory parade rolled past within a stone's throw of Gossard's London offices where the staff joined in the nation's salute to Winston Churchill. Buckingham Palace was floodlit again, the tradition of the Royal Garden Party returned and the Derby took place at Ascot. Whilst the house journals of the corsetry industry excitedly promised the arrival of new materials spawned by the wartime backroom scientist; nylon, a strong rigid yarn with great resilience and flexibility, had been produced from the by-products of coal and limestone (some even said it contained cod liver oil); Aralac, a wool substitute was made from casein found in cheese; Neoprene was a synthetic chemical product that stretched like rubber; glass fibre, mildew-proof, moth-proof, heat-proof and waterproof, made its debut; iridescent aluminium yarn and seaweed yarns promised brighter clothing.

The war was truly over and the future augured well.

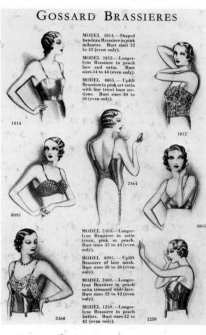

GOSSARD LINE OF BEAUTY

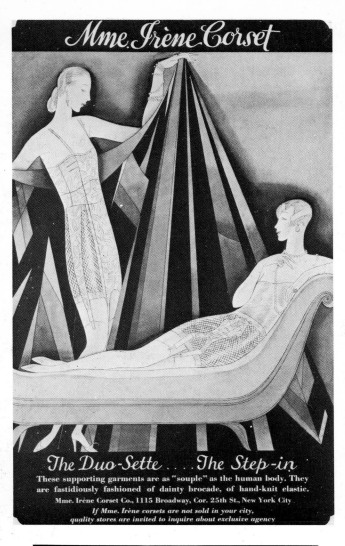

Mme. Irène Corset

The Duo-Sette .... The Step-in

These supporting garments are as "souple" as the human body. They
are fastidiously fashioned of dainty brocade, of hand-knit elastic.

Mme. Irène Corset Co., 1115 Broadway, Cor. 25th St., New York City

*If Mme. Irène corsets are not sold in your city,
quality stores are invited to inquire about exclusive agency*

Mme. Irène Corset

The "Duo-Sette"

The new modes are merciless in revealing figure deficiencies!
They demand a supporting garment—but its presence must not
be suspected! Show your patrons the Duo-Sette—a lovely union
of brassiere and ceinture—so easy and so satisfactory to sell!

Mme. Irène Corset Co., 1115 Broadway, Cor. 25th St., New York City

*If Mme. Irène Corsets are not sold in your city,
quality stores are invited to inquire about exclusive agency*

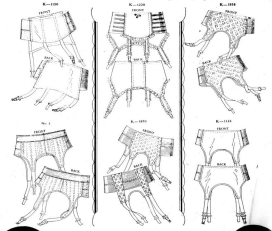
Came the 1930s and new words in
corsetry; the girdle and the step-in
made their appearance. The first to
control but lightly and support
stockings, the second to flatten and
suppress the female figure into the
popular boyish figure of emancipation.

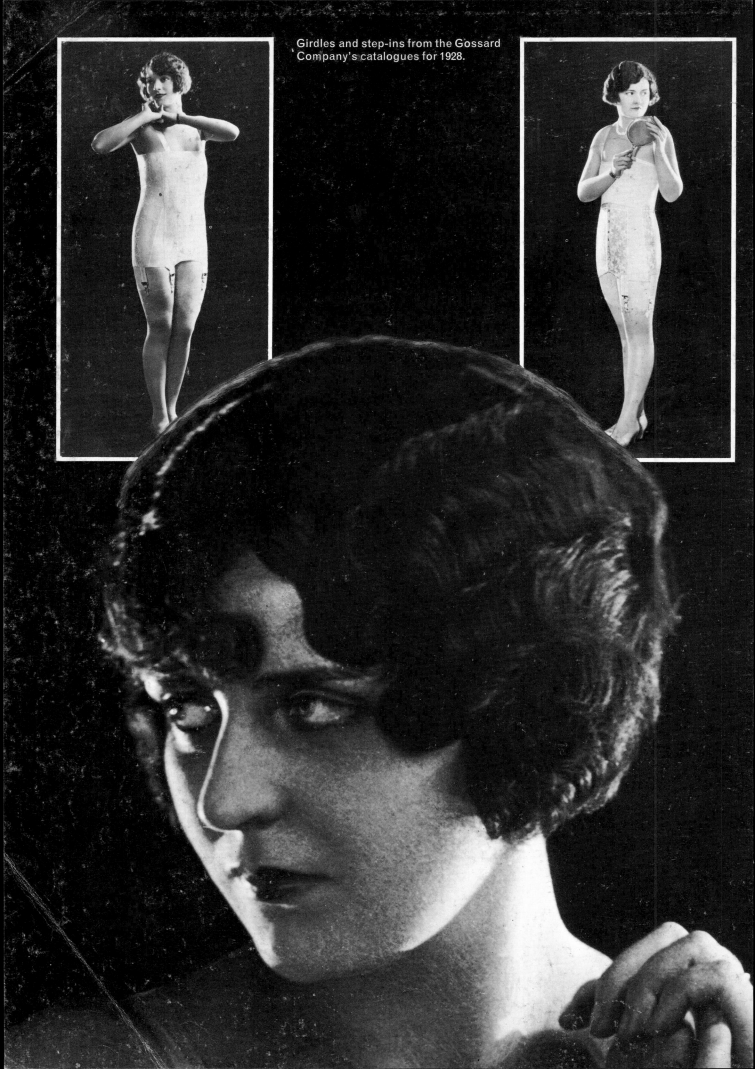

Girdles and step-ins from the Gossard
Company's catalogues for 1928.

Fifty years ago, but curiously
contemporary to the current catalogues
of leading underwear designers.

This cover, taken from a 1930s catalogue, reflects how the graphic artist brought art nouveau to the arcane world of corsetry.

1930 and the brassière and corset join
into 'combinations'. But sizing remains
divided into short, average and long
figures. The universal A, B, C, and D
cup sizes are still a few years away.

The Line of Beauty

GOSSARD
LINE OF BEAUTY

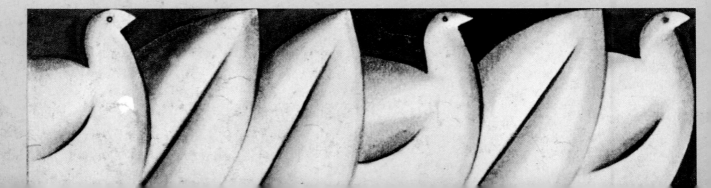

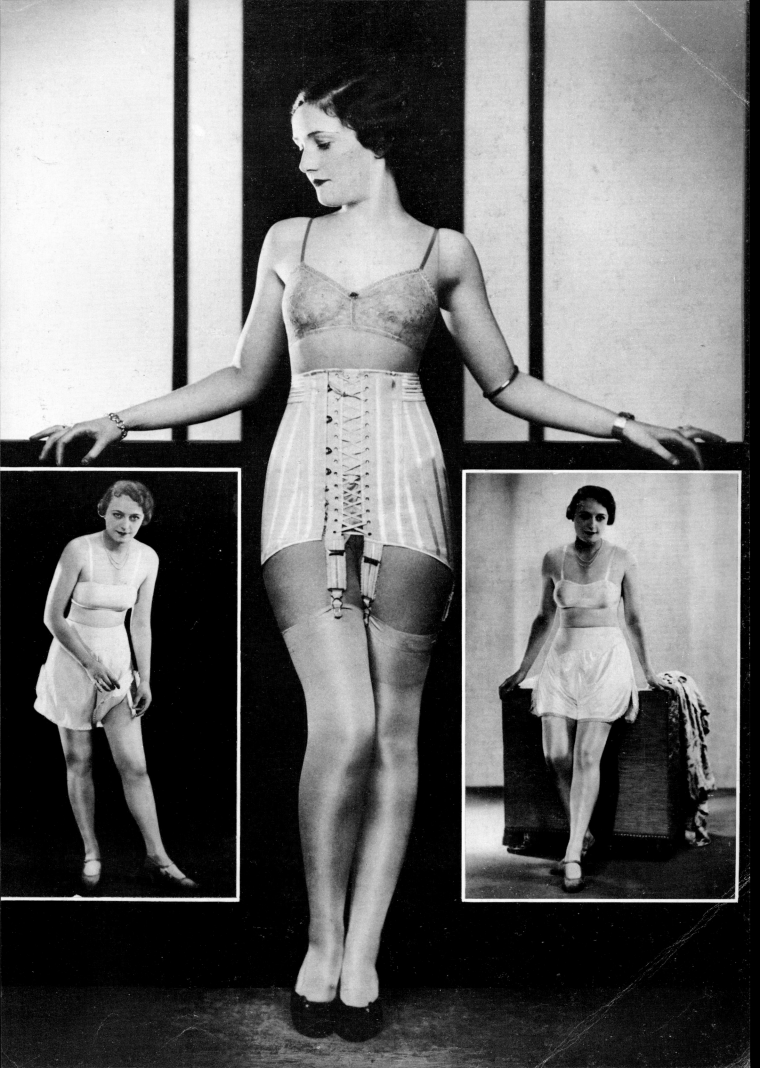

1936 and last ditch battles by the traditionalists in an attempt to fight off the new elastic fibre garments. This appeal, from I. Newman & Sons of New York City addressed to readers of a trade magazine, takes a defensive line in support of front lacing; 'Don't lose me in the Shuffle!'

1936 and trade buyers became excited over new designs from Maiden Form, jealously protected by patent and cunning – if cumbersome – in stitch design to meet fashion demands for a declared bust line.

HIGH NOTes for SPRING FASHIONS:

* *"VARIATION"

Maiden Form's latest brassiere creation, with front sections developed in an entirely new manner, to give a definite "dividing line" between the breasts, as well as extra-firm uplift support. "Variation" brassieres, with or without diaphragm bands—$8.00 and $12.00 a dozen. "Variation" "Once-Overs" (One-Piece Foundations)—$36.00 dozen.

* *"REMOLD"

Maiden Form's "Remold" brassieres solve the problem of the "sagging" or "pendulous" bust. An inner "shelf" of firm elastic serves to mould the breasts as well as to raise them to normal well-uplifted lines. $12.00 to $21.00 dozen.

* "OVER-TURE"

In the "Over-Ture" series of brassieres, Maiden Form first introduced under-breast stitching for extra-firm uplift support, in the form of little "petals." "Over-Ture" is still on the crest of its popularity! "Over-Ture" brassieres—$8.00 to $15.00 dozen.

* "INTER-LUDE"

By means of *semi-circular* under-breast stitching, Maiden Form's "Inter-Lude" brassieres give lovely classic rounded contours to the breast with a slight separation between—$8.00 to $36.00 dozen.

*"REMOLD"

*"VARIATION"

*"INTER-LUDE"

*"OVER-TURE"

DO YOU GET IT REGULARLY!— The Maiden Form Mirror (sent on request) gives *all* individual numbers and prices of these and other M. F. garments.

Maiden Form BRASSIERES
REG. U. S. PAT. OFF.
GIRDLES · GARTER BELTS

MAIDEN FORM BRASSIERE CO., INC., 200 MADISON AVE., NEW YORK

THE TRADE IS ADVISED THAT THE DESIGNS OF THESE MAIDEN FORM BRASSIERES ARE ALL FULLY PROTECTED BY PATENT

* Reg. U. S. Pat. Off.
* * Reg. App. for

On October 1 1931 the Warner Brothers Company launched a new type of corset. Le Gant was created from Lastex, a new elastic thread from the United States Rubber Company. Two way stretch had arrived and solved the problem of 'riding up'.

"Two Way-One Way"
LE GANT
The foundation that gives
CONTROL plus HINGE-ROOM

Back hips kept Flat and Smooth Garment always stays in place BECAUSE

Side Panels Stretch Both Ways

Center back Stretches Up and Down Only

THE WARNER BROTHERS CO., BRIDGEPORT, CONN.

For the corsetry industry on both sides of the Atlantic the war meant rescheduling production lines for the national effort. In America manufacturers like the Real-Form Girdle Company were making camouflage nets. In Britain Gossard were engaged in making parachutes, life belts, sails and flags but, as women formed an important part of the armed services, production of their underwear continued side by side with war contracts.

SAVED

...thanks to Camouflage Nets!

Wherever Allied fighting men serve the needs of war, camouflage nets...made by Real-Form ...are helping protect their lives and their mobile equipment. Camouflage nets...made on our Raschel knitting machines...along with a limited number of Real-Form girdles and panty girdles with lastex. • Both these forms of camouflage will be on display at our showrooms...during Corset Week. Come see them.

Real-Form
GIRDLES OF GRACE

REAL-FORM GIRDLE COMPANY, 358 FIFTH AVENUE, NEW YORK • MILL: BROOKLYN, NEW YORK

THE BODY UNLEASHED

THE FASHION WORLD TOOK even longer to recover from the second war than it had from the first. Paris was just as anxious to regain its leadership as it had been two decades earlier, and, in their first major post war showing, French designers attempted to repeat the Parisian style of the 1920s, thinly disguising it as the 'pencil line'. Schiaparelli declared: 'There is life and movement in the silhouette. The line is moulded with discretion giving an easy dignity to the figure'. Balenciaga declared for strapless décolleté, whilst Paquin offered tailored suits that had touches of 1880, and that old faithful—the Empire Line—was revived for evening wear.

This time the world was not so impressed. Britain's new young Queen continued to patronise her mother's designer Norman Hartnell, who, with a group of other British dress designers, was poised to open his salon. Paris tried valiantly to catch up, but even rising new talents like Christian Dior, who made clothes for Princess Margaret, could not match the determination of the London couturiers. A new era dawned when, during the fashion show of Edward Molyneux, the English designer working in the Rue de la Paix, a party from the British Embassy arrived. It was headed by the ambassador's wife, Lady Diana Duff Cooper, who eclipsed everyone in a London-inspired primrose satin evening-gown.

A further important influence was the discovery by British manufacturers that the volume of corsetry business in America had reached a figure of £45m; along with some exciting marketing ideas about special 'bra-bars' in department stores and the discovery of a recently identified group of young customers called 'teen-agers'. Manufacturers began, albeit haltingly, to attend to a clamouring domestic market, and at last British women were able to buy the new undergarments that had twinkled enticingly at them for so long from the fashion pages. Sales training was stepped up and assistants were told that, whilst the pre-war message had been 'The customer is always right', the new motto was more simply 'If you don't treat your customers right you won't have any customers left.'

Apart from deciding that the word brassière could now safely be abbreviated to 'bra', post-war America was learning to cope with the new materials spun-off by the war. Production problems in working the new nylon demanded special efforts. And then nylon was closely followed by Dacron which proved to be more absorbent of perspiration and more resistant to the contour changes brought about by body heat.

There were attempts to boost the bustline artificially after the fashion of the well-endowed film stars prompted by Hollywood's publicity machine. Early attempts were not always successful; one hapless flat-chested employee tested her company's artificial bust pads which were created from wire frames in the shape of miniature bird cages. Unhappily she wore them on an important first date and her report revealed that every time her escort let go of her she bounced off his chest. More successful attempts to help uplift the A-cup girl began with padded bras. Then came foam rubber inserts, removable for laundering, and made to resemble human flesh as closely as possible. One company even went so far as to promote its 'falsies' with an advertisement which was headed WE FIX FLATS!

The demand that immediately followed the war left the industry frantically trying to absorb returning personnel and the new materials generated as spin-offs of the war effort. And if these problems were not sufficient to tax their ingenuity there was the nervousness of the fashion world in seeking new styles. France lost its design lead to Hollywood's well-endowed film stars.

When fashion stipulated a high, emphasised bust, sales of bras soared and the designers were kept busy. Which came first, the strapless dress or the strapless bra is not clear, but with an improvement in strapless designing, many women who liked freedom over their shoulders began wearing strapless bras all the time with every style of dress. These were heady days for the manufacturers, but sales of the corset had dropped drastically: the offending garment was banished to the back of a girl's wardrobe, and it wasn't until Warners designed a 'combination cinch'—half bra and garter belt, called the 'Merry Widow' after a Hollywood movie—that sales of the corselette rallied.

fit your *Berlei* before your frock

With the new fabrics came a new approach to advertising. Madison Avenue devised such headlines as 'You ought to be hugged not squeezed' and 'How can you look so naughty and feel so nice' to accompany new photography in soft natural light. This put emphasis on beauty and grace, instead of the strictly practical concentration on every stitch of the garment.

The value of advertising also became apparent to British companies. In England Mrs Anne-Marie Lobbenberg, widow of one of Silhouette's founders, designed a corset with elastic which crossed the front of the garment in the shape of an 'x'. In 1955, with a modest turnover of £400,000 the company decided to gamble everything on this new product and emulate American techniques of promotion. By winning extended credit from its suppliers and a considerable bank overdraft, Silhouette took a deep breath, laced its corporate stays and allocated a massive £22,000 to advertising.

"UNDA LIFT" *Brassieres*

September 1956 saw the biggest advertising and promotional campaign in the history of British corsetry centred upon a leaping girl in a black leotard wearing the new 'Little X'. The company put 120,000 garments into the stores and for an agonising four weeks waited for retailers' reports. Then it started. Repeat orders came pouring in, customers cabled, telephone and wrote for more stocks and the factory was overwhelmed in production nightmares, but the gamble had worked. Within two months suppliers had been paid, the bank loan redeemed and, by the end of the year, turnover notched up by a half. The following year demand at home and abroad had grown to such an extent that licensing to manufacture 'Little X' had been granted in thirty-two countries including the United States. By 1959 Silhouette became a public company and such was the impact of its advertising campaign that the 450,000 ordinary shares on offer to the public were oversubscribed twenty-eight times.

McCall's Magazine bewailed the passing of that coveted prize of American feminity, 'the All-American girl', who 'until about twenty years ago [was] the best-dressed, prettiest female of the lot with by far the best legs. Now since the war, Europe and Asia have produced a crop of beauties who have snatched her crown. The girls in Sweden are breathtaking; the girls in Italy are ravishing; the girls in Germany sizzle and the girls in England fascinate'.

You'll look so naughty—feel so nice in WARNER'S

Merry Widow

WARNER'S

Bras · Girdles · Corselettes

Indeed, manufacturers on both sides of the Atlantic failed to see the fashionable *graffito*—a new generation was growing up, with-it kids of the cool beat scene who believed in jeans-with-everything. Corsetry was square to those in the groove. Fashion took the shape of a delightful young coltish model called Twiggy, and Carnaby Street finally eclipsed Paris as the centre of the fashion world, forcing even St Laurent to offer a beat look. He was no match, however, for such British designers as Mary Quant, Jeff Banks, Jean Muir, Ossie Clark, Zandra Rhodes and Bill Gibb.

The world's press clamoured to amaze their readers with the swinging London of the permissive era and such revelations as the mini-skirt, the jumpsuit and the bodystocking. A most important development in the world of underwear was also taking place; Janet Phillips, an award-winning student of the swimwear and foundation department of the world-famous Leicester College of Art, had been freelancing for a number of European manufacturers for some time before she met her German, scientist husband in Zurich.

The fateful marriage of Peter Reger's cautious Capricorn to Janet's luxurious Libra changed the world of women's underwear. In 1967 with a design consultancy in virtually every European capital the Euro-Rogers looked for a base to plant their own company. They chose Paris as an appropriate city to launch an international empire but it proved too costly, so it was to London that they moved from design consultancy to manufacture and retail, with Peter enthusiastically encouraging his wife to explore and proclaim the inherent sexual sensuality of feminine underwear.

In rediscovering luxury, Janet Reger abolished the traditional concept that underwear was somehow unmentionable, occupying a position vaguely between shoes and outerwear. She created beautiful garments which delighted their owners and made them feel special, with the result that her designs became appreciated by men and women alike, although not everyone can afford the luxury she offers.

The end of the sixties brought a last permissive convulsion in the shape of unfettered bosoms, prompted by the militant growth of women's liberation movements in all corners of the globe. To the delight of the tabloids, and the consternation of the manufacturers, bra-burning enjoyed a flaming explosion and spotting bra-less women became a popular male spectator sport.

The bra-less period proved relatively short-lived, but another innovation, tights or pantyhose, soon made roll-on girdles unnecessary as a means of holding stockings up. The dramatic decline in sales of the roll-on worried both garment manufacturers and their textile suppliers; in 1975 Du Pont, creators of Lycra and godmother to the industry, commissioned three research studies to probe the problem. Hundreds of women across America were interviewed and thousands of pages of material gathered for analysis.

The answers were depressing. The reports showed that there had always been a resentment towards girdles, women disliked the restriction and discomfort but wore girdles in spite of it, there seemed no option. Some women believed that they caused physical problems: 'They make your muscles flabby and cause varicose veins.' 'My gynaecologist told me to diet and exercise. He told me never to wear a girdle again.' It soon became apparent that changing life-styles and attitudes to dress had helped to make the girdle obsolete. To many women, who were now learning to be their natural selves, the element of deception involved in wearing such restrictive foundation garments seemed like cheating. Other women considered them a symbol of male chauvinism: 'What would men say if we asked *them* to wear a girdle?' And it became obvious that men didn't like the feel of unyielding rigidity where there should be flesh. Above all, women didn't want to admit that they were out of shape; 'If I have to wear a girdle, that tells me I am getting old, that I'm aging.'

Embarrassingly the reports also indicated that the industry had made the problems worse by advertising the product as though it were a remedy, without showing how it could make women look and feel better. The very word 'girdle' conjured up the antithesis of the kind of clothing that women wanted; bulky, lumpy,

uncomfortable, restricting, old-fashioned.

A new image was needed and one which would convey the idea of a garment which was soft, flexible, flowing, yielding, fun, sensuous, sexual, healthy, sporting, natural, casual and colourful. The name 'bodygarment' emerged and new designs were explored. Du Pont called in one of the fashion industry's top designers, Rudi Gernreich, originator of the topless swimsuit.

Alongside this major rethink of the shape of foundation garments has come fresh information about the female shape. In the UK in 1978 Berlei announced the preliminary findings of their anthropological survey of British women. From a very detailed questionnaire of 5000 women aged between 18 and sixty-five it is clear that better nutrition and the widespread use of the oral contraceptive pill have undoubtedly changed the shape of woman— over 46 per cent now wear a B-size cup whilst a further 17 per cent wear a C-cup. Further statistics show that bras are being worn at increasingly younger ages; 7 per cent of those interviewed wore their first bra at the age of 11; 18 per cent at 12 and 22 per cent at 13, thus indicating a far larger market in teenage garments than many manufacturers may have appreciated.

Thanks to Berlei we now know that Ms Average British stands 5ft 3in weighs 9st 2lbs and measures 35.9in : 27.8in. : 38.1in. Thanks also to Sears, Roebuck, the US mail order giant, who revised their design patterns in 1978 we know that Ms-size-10-America measures 34.5in. : 26in. : 36.5in., which helps us create a revealing table:

THE CHANGING SHAPE OF WOMEN

	BUST	WAIST	HIPS	HEIGHT
Venus de Milo	34in.	31.2in.	40.8in.	5ft.4in.
1925 Survey of American Beauty Queens	34in.	26in.	35in.	5ft.4in.
1978 Sears Roebuck design changes (size 10)	34.5in.	26in.	36.5in.	n/a
1978 Berlei UK survey	35.9in.	27.8in.	38.1in.	5ft.3in.

n/a: not available

The plaster model, the corsetry manufacturers stock in trade.

Of course 'average' figures notoriously absorb contrasts such as the geographical differences in body shapes even within the United States; women on the Eastern seaboard have smaller bosoms than their West-Coast sisters whilst garment sales prove they have wider hips.

But what these figures do reveal is that the blossoming female shape is not entirely due to the Pill alone; they underline the fact that having suffered centuries of rigid figure torture, women have finally abandoned whalebone and wadding in favour of muscle control and see-through fabrics.

TOTAL
HEIGHT

TOTAL HEIGHT 161cm (5'3")

SHOULDER HEIGHT 152cm (4'2")

CIRCUMFERENCE
OF THORAX

BUST
CIRCUMFERENCE

BUST HEIGHT 115cm (3'9½")

UNDER-BUST
CIRCUMFERENCE

UNDER-BUST HEIGHT 114cm (3'9")

INTER-NIPPLE
DISTANCE

WAIST
CIRCUMFERENCE

WAIST HEIGHT 98cm (3'2¾")

ABDOMINAL PROJECTION HEIGHT 93cm (3'0¾")

HIP
CIRCUMFERENCE

CIRCUMFERENCE
OF BOTH LEGS

KNEE HEIGHT 46cm (1'6¼")

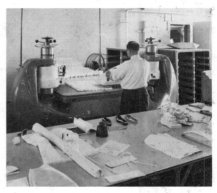

Amazingly a standard line – like this 'Lifestyle' bra from Silhouette, one of Britain's top manufacturers requires 26 components, the most painstaking cutting and endless machinings before it is packed for despatch.

The 1950s found corsetry
manufacturers freed from the
restrictions of wartime utility
production and eager to return to the
growth of competitive trading.
Gossard found no shortage of
promotional ideas. *Above,* a contest to
discover amateur models in a much
neglected area of fashion and, *left,* a
presentation to members of the Royal
Ballet Company.

1950 and the trade fair at London's Park Lane Hotel gives a thumbs down to the discreet white garments of the immediate post-war years and dives into black, with a sally into the Polynesian. The main illustration reveals a black tulle brassière by Mador of Paris with a nylon two-way stretch belt in power net.

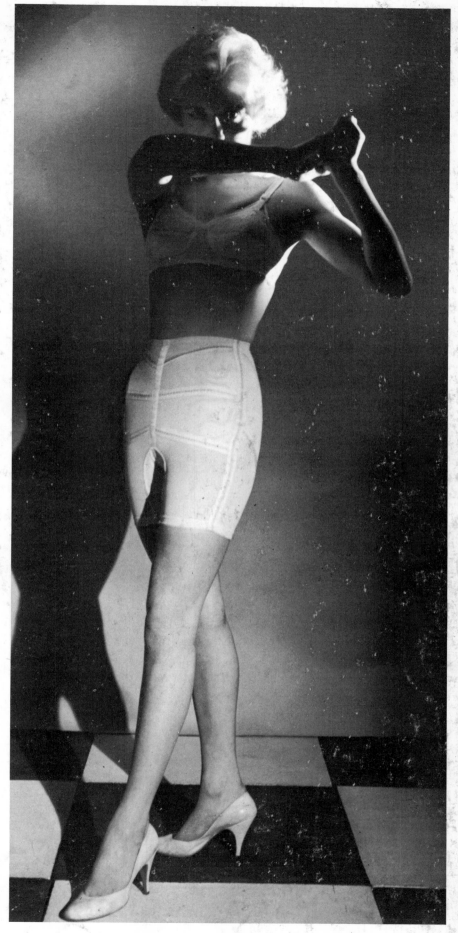

Facing page : 1951 and a new fashion era begins with Warner's Merry Widow a combination cinch, half-brassière and garter belt designed to be worn with tight-waisted bare topped dresses. Inspiration for this garment came from the release of a Lana Turner movie version of Franz Lehar's 'Merry Widow' operetta.

This page : Attempts to anticipate fashion trends; the detachable halter, backless and long leg panties.

Into the 1960s and with the aid of new stretch fabrics like Lycra from Du Pont, plus a deliberate fashion attempt to appeal to the high-income younger woman the industry strove to combine design and appeal.

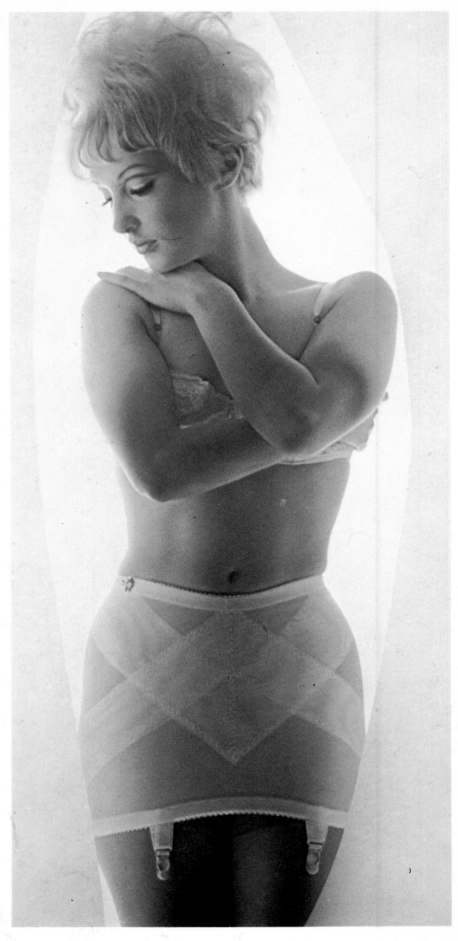

The concept of corsetry was square to
the groovy with-it kids of the cool beat
scene who marked the mass jeans-
with-everything youthful explosion of
the swinging sixties. But the industry
fought back valiantly with such
devices as front-fastening, pretty
styles and careful attention to shape
enhancement, as these pages and the
two that follow clearly show.

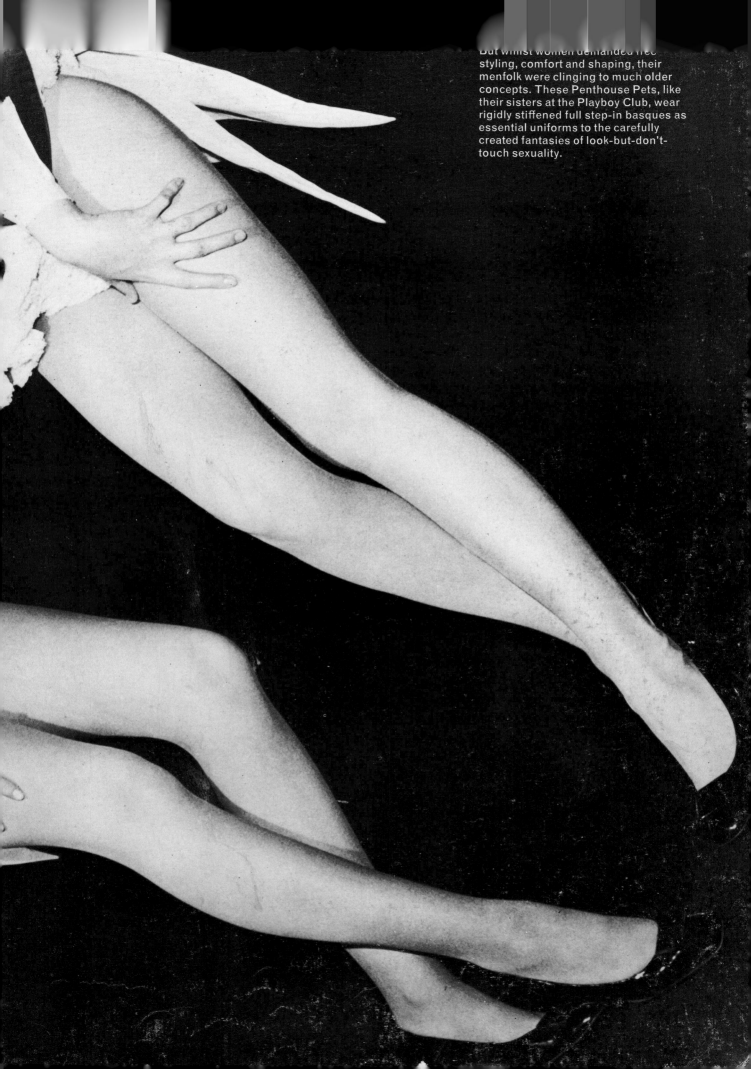

But whilst women demanded free styling, comfort and shaping, their menfolk were clinging to much older concepts. These Penthouse Pets, like their sisters at the Playboy Club, wear rigidly stiffened full step-in basques as essential uniforms to the carefully created fantasies of look-but-don't-touch sexuality.

The late sixties and for the first time men begin to appear in underwear advertising campaigns. The permissive era opened many such doors.

The swinging sixties. Photographer David Bailey's interpretation of a popular bra from Gossard, appropriately called 'Jet Set'.

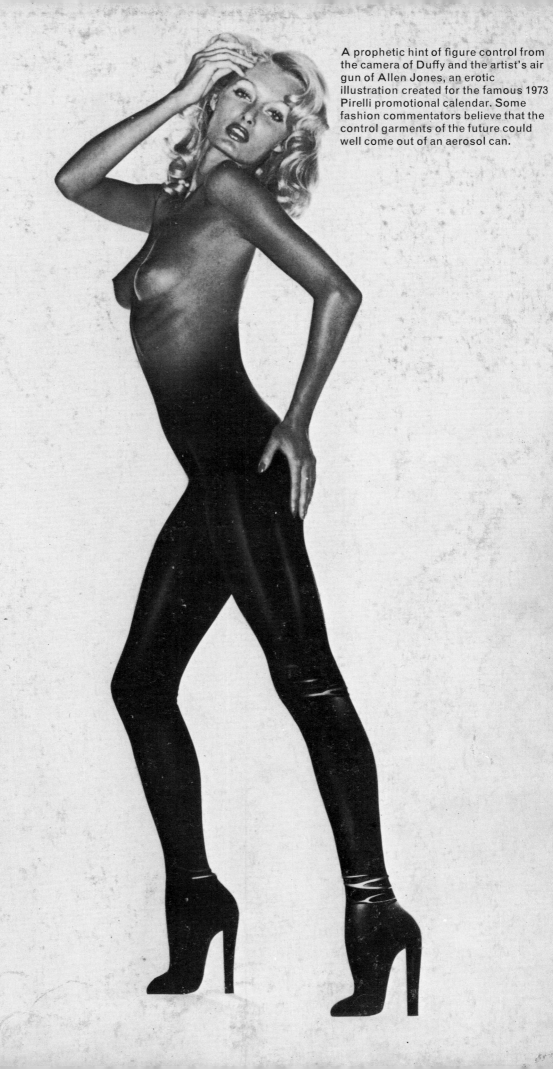

A prophetic hint of figure control from the camera of Duffy and the artist's air gun of Allen Jones, an erotic illustration created for the famous 1973 Pirelli promotional calendar. Some fashion commentators believe that the control garments of the future could well come out of an aerosol can.

The beginning of the seventies saw a new natural look in outer fashion. Energetically recovering from the short-lived bra-burning late sixties the underwear industry responded with lighter weight, softer and thinner garments. Function bowed towards appeal and the arrival of the see-through bra.

In an attempt to revitalise the staid, matronly image of corsetry, killing off words like 'girdle' in favour of 'control garments' the designers made concerted efforts to relate underwear to outerwear, These co-ordinated garments appeared at fashion shows in Britain and Germany in 1978.

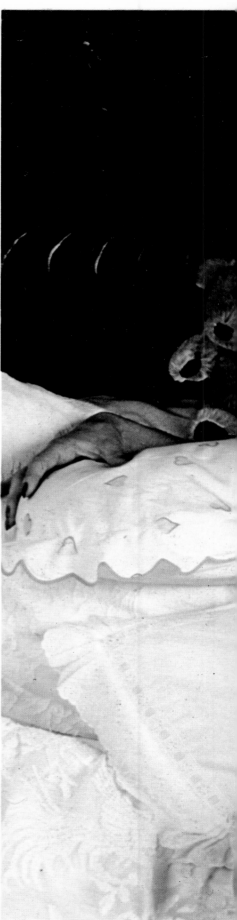

Undoubtedly one of the best-known designer names in underwear fashion is Janet Reger who set out to create beautiful garments that would make women feel special.

In rediscovering the female body Janet
Reger – discreetly aided and
encouraged by her husband Peter –
erased those traditional concepts that
underwear lay somewhere vaguely
between shoes and outerwear. As
Janet Phillips she had been an award
winning student of the swimwear and
foundation department of the world
famous Leicester College of Art before
freelancing as a designer for a number
of European manufacturers. The
Regers launched their own company in
London in 1967 and rapidly won
international acclaim. These pages and
the four that follow reveal just how
much Janet Reger has explored and
proclaimed the inherent sexual
sensuality of feminine underwear and
help to explain just why her creations
are so highly prized.

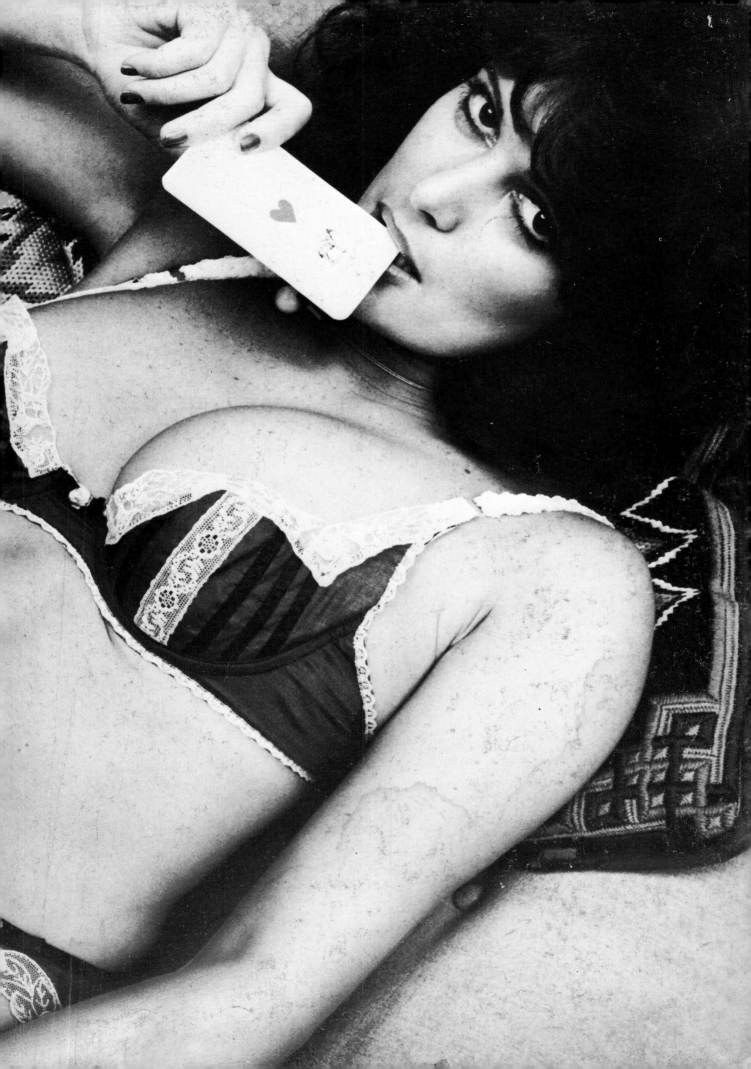

'Glossies', the underwear success
story of the 1970s.
Created by Lily of France,
these shimmering, moulded see-
through garments won instant
acclaim in America, a success story
that was repeated by Gossard in
Britain. One of the lightest and,
according to customers, one of the
most comfortable mass-manufactured
designs to hit the international market.

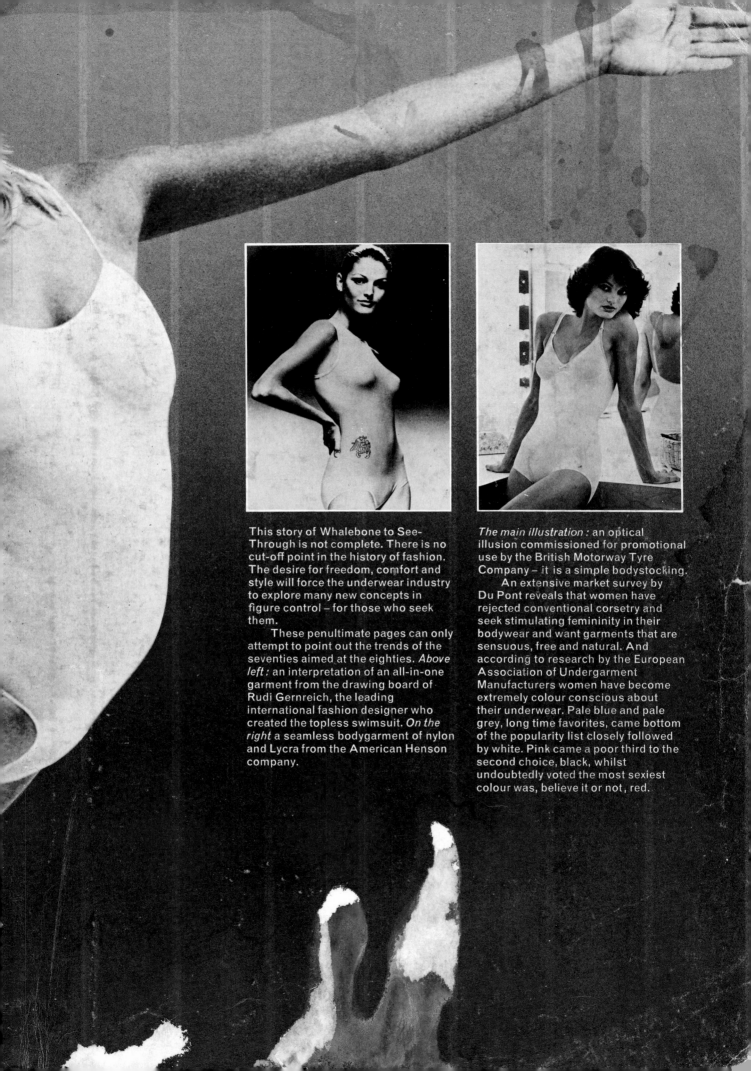

This story of Whalebone to See-Through is not complete. There is no cut-off point in the history of fashion. The desire for freedom, comfort and style will force the underwear industry to explore many new concepts in figure control – for those who seek them.

These penultimate pages can only attempt to point out the trends of the seventies aimed at the eighties. *Above left :* an interpretation of an all-in-one garment from the drawing board of Rudi Gernreich, the leading international fashion designer who created the topless swimsuit. *On the right* a seamless bodygarment of nylon and Lycra from the American Henson company.

The main illustration : an optical illusion commissioned for promotional use by the British Motorway Tyre Company – it is a simple bodystocking.

An extensive market survey by Du Pont reveals that women have rejected conventional corsetry and seek stimulating femininity in their bodywear and want garments that are sensuous, free and natural. And according to research by the European Association of Undergarment Manufacturers women have become extremely colour conscious about their underwear. Pale blue and pale grey, long time favorites, came bottom of the popularity list closely followed by white. Pink came a poor third to the second choice, black, whilst undoubtedly voted the most sexiest colour was, believe it or not, red.